Interethnic Communication

Ron Scollon
Suzanne B.K. Scollon

Interethnic Communication

Ron Scollon
Suzanne B.K. Scollon

Alaska Native Language Center
University of Alaska Fairbanks
1980

First Printing, 1980	500 copies
Second Printing, 1981	300 copies
Third Printing, 1982	300 copies
Fourth Printing, 1983	300 copies
Fifth Printing, 1984	500 copies
Sixth Printing, 1986	300 copies
Seventh Printing, 1986	500 copies
Eighth Printing, 1987	500 copies
Ninth Printing, 1988	1,000 copies
Tenth Printing, 1990	1,000 copies
Eleventh Printing, 1994	1,000 copies

Contents

Introduction

This booklet is designed as background material to accompany "Interethnic Communication," a videotape in the series "Talking Alaska," also available through the Alaska Native Language Center. Portions of this booklet were prepared for use in our presentation at the annual Alaska Bilingual-Mulitcultural Education Conference in 1979 and 1980. Some of that material and other portions have also appeared as a regular column in the Alaska Court System Newsletter. We have prepared this booklet and the accompanying videotape because many people have requested them for personal use and for use in workshops and other presentations on cross-cultural and interethnic communication.

The most important aspect of interethnic communication is that it is <u>inter-ethnic</u>. That is, for the users of this material to understand fully the issues raised here, they must be in communication with members of different ethnic groups, and not just in communication, but in communication *about* communication. In our recommendations at the end, we suggest ways in which users can make further steps toward improving interethnic communication.

We hope this material will help users learn about problems of interethnic communication. This could be useful in workshops and inservice training sessions, especially where communication *between* ethnic groups is encouraged. We want to caution, however, that understanding these issues is difficult and comes slowly. No one using this material should expect either the booklet itself or the videotape or any limited-time training session to do any more than point the way to the problem. If this material helps the users begin to see where negative personal and ethnic stereotypes come from and how central the problem of stereotyping is to societal problems of discrimination against ethnic and other minorities, it will serve its purpose.

Suggestions for Use of This Material

We have tried to prepare this booklet and the accompanying video tape for multiple uses. The videotape has been broadcast by satellite television without this booklet and has been reasonably successful. Most of the materials in this booklet have been made available to people who did not have the videotape, and the response has also been favorable. We suggest then that the user will be able to profit from flexible use of these materials. The suggestions we give here should be understood as only an indication of how we ourselves sometimes use this material.

If this material is used for inservice training or workshops, there are several things you might think about first.

1. Preparation

When participants in a training session have some idea of what to expect before the session begins, they generally make more sense out of the actual training activities. Unfortunately, advance preparation also gives participants an opportunity to build up their defenses against learning something that might be personally threatening. Advance preparation, on the other hand, gives people a chance to think out their own positions so that they will be able to speak and think more clearly about them in the training session itself.

Our goal is to help people understand their positions, and so we believe that the sooner this process of understanding begins, the better.

Three kinds of advance preparation may be important. The first is the orientation of the participants to the purposes of the training, who will be conducting the training, why they are being involved in it, and what they are expected to get out of it. One way this orientation can be done is by asking participants to read the background selection (at least) of this booklet, and by circulating in advance a general description of the planned training.

A second, more important kind of advance preparation is an analysis of the problem by the parties planning and giving the training. Training in interethnic communication is not trivial and it is not easy. It involves some of the deepest personal, social, political and economic issues in the contemporary world. Any training that does not acknowledge this fact can produce more harm than good. If participants, including planners and trainers, can tell themselves after a workshop that they've "done interethnic communication" and have nothing further to be worried about, they have failed to understand how serious an issue it is. Advance planning at this level includes thinking about what deep-seated difficulties can be expected to surface among the expected participants, and how they will be dealt with as they surface.

The most important level of advance preparation is the third. We feel that it is essential to involve members of all of the relevant ethnic groups in the *first* stages of planning. This will help to incorporate varied points of view into the original issues of setting goals and expectations. Differences in communicative styles will be reflected in different views about how one conducts teaching and learning, and these differences must be addressed as soon as possible. These differences should also be reflected in the agenda(s) of the training session.

2. Initial Session

We feel it is best to open any training session with an opportunity for all participants to voice their interests and concerns. Even though the main concern may be to have the presenters get on with a formal presentation, it is best to allow participants to voice them.

There are a few important aspects of an initial session. One is that while all participants should be allowed the opportunity to voice their concerns, we feel that <u>no participant should be required to do so</u>. Since some people feel more comfortable than others with giving their names and identifying themselves, this identification should be done by some means such as giving name tags or listing participants in a program. Individuals should not be made to identify themselves if they choose not to do so.

The opening discussion should include participants from all relevant ethnic groups. One should take care that all points of view are represented if this can be done without forcing any participant to speak when they choose not to.

If it is possible to tape-record this session, the presenters will find many instances of stereotyped interethnic communicative behavior that can be used later for analysis and understanding. Presenters will also find that they themselves will contribute many negative examples. These are the best to use as illustrations because the presenter will not be exposing other participants to embarrassment and at the same time be showing willingness to examine openly his own communicative style. (If any recordings are to be made, it is essential to gain permission in advance from all participants.)

This initial session could be guided with a few key topics:

a. Individual differences and ethnic differences. Is it possible to say a certain behavior or way of doing something or speaking is "ethnic?" How can you make generalizations if members of the same group are often very different from each other?

b. The dangers of generalization. Are people really all just the same? Or are they all different? How can we best understand both the similarities and the differences among people? How can we talk about differences without implying negative attitudes toward those differences? How can we talk about similarities without erasing distinctive individual qualities of people?

c. The purposes of communication. Is communication primarily about ideas or relationships? Is it necessary to speak a certain language or in a certain way to be a member of a certain ethnic group?

d. Definition of "ethnic group." How can you tell that someone is a member of an ethnic group? Do members of an ethnic group identify their own members in the same way that outsiders do? Do all members of a group identify in the same way or to the same extent? Who gets to decide who is a member of an ethnic group? The individual? The government? Does it make a difference who decides?

These discussion topics might help to get participants to think about the issues of inter-ethnic communication. There are many other issues, and each one could take a long time to discuss. We offer these only as suggestions. If these topics were given to participants as advance preparation, it might help them start thinking about them before the initial session.

The initial session should continue for as long as participants feel they are learning something about themselves and each other. Presenters should never feel they have the answers and cut off the initial discussion too soon. The advance preparation, the videotape and the other planned activities are the presenter's contribution to the discussion, but this is only one person or group's contribution and should be balanced by contributions of the other participants. Presenters should be ready to alter the planned agenda if the current participants prefer another.

3. Videotape presentation

It is not necessary to give any introduction to the tape "Interethnic Communication." If there is time or if the presenters choose to do so, it might be useful to review the contents of the film. This review should be kept brief.

Points that should be made are:

a. Athabaskan-English interethnic communication is only one example of many that could have been chosen to make this tape.

b. Neither side should be taken as the "good guys" or the "bad guys." What is important is that they approach the situation differently and may misunderstand each other.

c. The scenes in the videotape are play-acted by non-professional actors to illustrate points. We do not believe that all Athabaskans act just like Mrs. Smith in the tape or that all Whites act just like Mr. Brown. We do believe that something like this happens pretty often to members of many different groups and can influence the economic mobility of the minority participant.

d. Even though we tried to illustrate negative interactions in the role-played scenes and positive ones in the discussion, you will notice places where we didn't really get together even when we tried. This will illustrate that it is very difficult to alter one's basic patterns of communicative style, even with the best of intentions.

4. Discussion of the videotape

In our experience, direct discussion of the videotape is difficult. People often prefer to think about it on their own. You should take care not to force a discussion where it is not moving naturally. If you do decide to discuss the tape, it often works best to take a break just after viewing the tape and begin the discussion after the break. This will give any participants for whom discussion is embarrassing a chance to leave.

Discussion should move as freely as possible <u>among topics raised by participants</u>. It is important to find out what the viewers saw and how they responded and not to impose your view on them. Many participants may be sensitive to patterns of turn-changing and interruptions just after seeing this videotape. You might have an opportunity to build on this sensitivity. Watch for group awareness of some speakers dominating others by taking turns too rapidly, but do not embarrass individuals who have been cut off by then forcing them to speak.

You should be cautioned that this sort of discussion can be uncomfortable for you to do and also for the participants. That can be used as an important point if it is done carefully. We often fail to come to grips with communicative difficulty because it is uncomfortable to do so. This is the best and maybe the only time to raise these issues directly with participants.

Again, if this discussion can be tape-recorded, it might provide useful examples for later study and discussion. (Be certain to get permission for recording from the participants.)

Other key topics:

a. How is the job interview different from other interviews such as a visit to the doctor? How about a committee meeting or teaching a class to adults or children? How is it like or unlike making an arrest or being arrested? How is it like your workshop?

b. What could Mr. Brown and Mrs. Smith have done differently? Could they really have done it? Try to be realistic about suggestions. If unrealistic suggestions are made, try to discuss why they couldn't work.

c. How could the videotape have been done differently to illustrate these points or other points better?

5. Post-workshop evaluation

In our experience, what people say at the end of a training session or right after does not really mean very much. People don't really know what they have learned until they have a chance to get back into the real world and try it out. We recommend that if post-workshop evaluations are needed, they be done about six months after the training session is completed. We recommend interviews if possible, but if not, a questionnaire can sometimes be useful. These should be brief and open-ended. What you want to know is if participants were able to make sense of anything in their own private and public or professional lives because of their participation in the training. Often participants will feel they have learned most from other participants, not from the "official" presenter. That is a very good outcome, so be careful not to bias your evaluation against that sort of statement. Also, be especially open to negative comments. These are sometimes the best indication that natural and voluntary change in communicative patterns is taking place.

The results of this evaluation can be very useful in further training. They can also be very useful to us and we would appreciate any feedback on the use of these materials or suggested ways in which they could be improved.

6. Time considerations

This booklet can be read in a short time, and the videotape is approximately thirty minutes long. Obviously the rest of the time in the training session will be used in activities created or directed by the presenters and the participants. We feel that the open discussion among participants of different ethnic groups is the critical dimension of any training that would use these materials. The suggested uses given here are based on a three-hour continuous session.

Basic Principles
of Interethnic Communication

1. The Importance of Communication

People from different ethnic groups often have different ways of communicating. In face-to-face communication these differences in language, communicative style or ways of speaking can become cumulative and even result in discrimination against ethnic and other minorities. Difficulties arise because people do not understand a different style of communicating, and then people might jump to the wrong conclusions. Sometimes these wrong conclusions are the result of different ways of using a language in oral communication. These ways of speaking, which make up the communicative style of a particular individual or ethnic group, are independent of an individual's degree of education. In fact, the most highly educated member of ethnic minorities are often faced with more discrimination than less educated members.

Recently there has been much research into the cultural and linguistic conventions that affect communicative style. The ways in which the organization of an argument or an unexpected tone of voice can cause misunderstanding in cross-cultural or interethnic communication have been studied. The ethnic stereotypes that are the result of miscommunication can be overcome if we realize that the aspects of communicative style that are misinterpreted are not intentional but habitual, that they do not reflect bad attitudes but are simply a part of the cultural or ethnic upbringing of the person.

Communication most often breaks down, not in relaxed situations among friends, but in situations of stress such as job or welfare interviews, arrests, counseling interviews or other similar situations. These situations have been called "gatekeeping encounters." At these times, participants are not likely to be aware of what is causing the problem, and attempts to repair the situation might only make matters worse.

We realize that ethnic discrimination is undoubtedly a political and economic matter to a great extent. At the same time, though, we must realize that political and economic affairs are largely carried out in situations of face-to-face communications. Many people have thought that education of ethnic minorities would reduce problems of discrimination. On the other hand, it is often assumed that educating non-minority group members to the ways of ethnic minorities will also end discrimination. Because communication is so central to all aspects of modern life, unless people are aware of what and how they are communicating even without intending to, much of this education might not be as profitable as expected. These misunderstandings are often found within the very agencies that are supposed to be providing equal opportunities, because of a general lack of awareness of the role of communicative style in creating personal and ethnic stereotypes.

There are three basic steps toward improving interethnic communication.

Perception: We need to perceive that our communication is not entirely successful.

Acceptance: We need to accept that others do not intend to convey wrong or confusing information or to convey negative attitudes.

Repair: We need to seek ways of explicitly sorting out how and where our communication goes wrong.

The purpose of this booklet and the videotape it accompanies is to help you in the first two steps, to see that there might be a problem of communication, even where everyone involved has the best of intentions, and to help you to accept that where others appear to be acting negatively, it might be a more basic problem of miscommunication.

We also want to emphasize how difficult the third step is. We have all been brought up to communicate in specific ways. We unconsciously feel that our own way of communicating is natural and correct and that any deviations from this style are unusual or strange. As we begin to notice our own style in relationship to others, our first reaction might be to condemn the communicative style of the others. This is because our own communicative style is a critical part of our own cultural, ethnic, and personal sense of identity. As some individuals go even further and try to make changes in their own styles, they find that they just can't do it. It has taken many years to learn one's own style and it will take many more to change it. For this reason, we are not suggesting that this material will help anyone change their own communicative style. Many users will choose not to do so. We do hope that it will help you to realize how your own communicative style might be communicating things you do not intend to communicate to others. Our goal is to help you come to a better understanding of your own ways of communicating and the effect your style has on others.

2. Interethnic Communication in Alaska

When we think of interethnic communication in Alaska, we usually think first of communication between Alaska Natives and members of one of the newly arrived groups of non-Native colonists and settlers, especially Americans. It is important to realize, though, that there are many different ethnic and cultural groups native to Alaska. We cannot make generalizations about "Alaska Natives" and hope that they will be fair to very many individuals. We know that there are some twenty different Native languages in Alaska and that conversation between people who speak these languages is a significant aspect of contemporary Alaskan public life. On the other hand, not all Americans are members of the same ethnic or language groups. Among Americans there are many ethnic groups, often with distinctive communicative styles and traditions.

The ethnic composition of present-day Alaska presents a very complicated picture with as many as fifty different groups in large urban centers and with at least several groups represented in most smaller settlements. As a result, interethnic communication is a daily experience for most residents of the state.

We are concerned with negative ethnic stereotypes that develop in communication between members of different ethnic groups and with finding ways to break down these stereotypes. In order to give as realistic details as possible, we are going to begin with just one example, Athabaskan-English interethnic communication. The principles involved can be found working in many other kinds of situations. We find similar things going on in communication between two members of the same ethnic groups, whether they are Native or non-Native. In those cases the negative stereotypes are held about individuals as personalities rather than as members of ethnic groups.

It is difficult to talk about communication between Athabaskans and speakers of English. There are no good words to refer to the two groups we are talking about. By "Athabaskan" we mean anyone who has been brought up with a set of communicative patterns that have their roots in the Athabaskan languages. On the whole, these people are ethnically Athabaskan, but they might not speak any Athabaskan language. By "speakers of English" we mean anyone whose communicative patterns are those of the dominant mainstream American, English-speaking population. Many of these are not racially or ethnically white. We know this is awkward since most of the communication we are looking at is English. It seems better than using a term like Standard English, which seems to suggest that one variety of English is to be preferred over another. We also realize that there are many individual differences among people, even where they identify as members of a particular group. We still feel that the patterns we will describe here hold true in a general way and are the patterns on which people have developed ethnic stereotypes. Because of the consistency of these ethnic stereotypes, we feel there is a consistent pattern of discourse underlying this stereotyping. We are aware of the dangers of making generalizations but are also aware that saying that all people are just the same in communicative style creates a dangerous potential for discrimination against ethnic minorities.

3. Ethnic Stereotyping: Some problems in Athabaskan-English interethnic communication

Most of us are aware of racial and ethnic stereotypes. White speakers of English in Alaska often think of Athabaskans as quiet or even withdrawn. They might think that Athabaskans do not want to get along with others. Athabaskans might think of English speakers as boastful, domineering and too talkative.

Ethnic stereotypes of the silent Indian or the domineering white man do not come out of nowhere. They might result in attitudes that are unjustified, for in many cases the conversational partners know each other well and think highly of each other. They might nevertheless find that they are stereotyping each other on the basis of patterns of discourse. If we can understand what causes these ethnic stereotypes, we might be able to adjust the way we speak so that we do not offend people of the other ethnic group with whom it is important for us to get along.

Ethnic stereotypes are related to patterns of behavior and ways of speaking that we learn when we are young. Indian children learn to respect their elders by keeping silent in their presence. White American children learn to talk to their parents, to show off what they can say and do. From these basic differences comes much of the confusion that results when the two groups come together. Negative ethnic stereotypes are the result of this confusion.

If we look at what confuses people when Athabaskans and English speakers talk together, we might be able to understand how the confusion comes about.

What's confusing to English speakers about Athabaskans	What's confusing to Athabaskans about English speakers
The presentation of self	
They do not speak	They talk too much
They keep silent	They always talk first
They avoid situations of talking	They talk to strangers or people they don't know
They only want to to talk to close acquaintances	They think they can predict the future
They play down their own abilities	They brag about themselves
They act as if they expect things to be given to them	They don't help people even when they can
They deny planning	They always talk about what's going to happen later
The distribution of talk	
They avoid direct questions	They ask too many questions
They never start a conversation	They always interrupt
They talk off the topic	They only talk about what they are interested in
They never say anything about themselves	They don't give others a chance to talk
They are slow to take a turn in talking	They just go on and on when they talk

What's confusing to English speakers about Athabaskans	What's confusing to Athabaskans about English speakers
The contents of talk	
They are too indirect, too inexplicit	They aren't careful when they talk about people or things
They don't make sense	
They just leave without saying anything	They have to say 'goodbye' even when they can see that you are leaving

There are three kinds of problems here. The first is what we call the presentation of self. When we talk, we present a view of ourselves to each other. English speakers enjoy talking with different people who might change their perspective on life. Only with people they know well do they think there is no need to talk. Athabaskans, on the other hand, enjoy talking with people they know well who share their point of view. In situations where they do not know each other, even in cases where parents and children have been separated for some time, they prefer not to talk much until they know where they stand with each other. They have a high degree of respect for each other's individuality, which they demonstrate by not talking too much or asking too many questions. In this way they preserve their own individual points of view. Athabaskans value getting to know each other by observing people's actions. English speakers value conversation as a way of getting to know people.

Now we can see that if two people who do not know each other meet, the English speaker will want to talk so that they can get to know each other, but the Athabaskan will want to wait until they know each other before feeling comfortable in speaking.

When we talk to people, we want to know who is dominant in the relationship between speakers, or, in other words, who is in the position of higher status. This relationship determines who will do most of the talking. For American English speakers, the person in the dominant position asks questions and then listens while the subordinate person shows off what he knows by talking. Children often entertain parents and seek to please teachers by talking.

For Athabaskans, children are supposed to be quiet. They learn by listening to and observing adults, who display abilities and qualities that are valued in their culture. This difference in behavioral expectations can cause confusion in educational settings where the teacher is a non-Athabaskan English speaker and the students are Athabaskan. The teacher expects the children to display their knowledge in class while remaining in the dominant role as the teacher. The children, when asked to speak up, think the tables have been turned and become unruly in the eyes of the teacher. To the children, the teacher will seem incompetent if he doesn't lecture a lot, or will seem bossy if he acts superior to the children in spite of not doing most of the talking. The Athabaskan teacher who expects the children to observe him carefully in class might seem to his English-speaking colleagues to be doing no teaching.

In conversation between an English teacher and an Athabaskan, the same confusion exists. If the English speaker does most of the speaking, he interprets the Athabaskan's silence as displaying superiority. The Athabaskan in turn feels that the English speaker in being so talkative is acting superior. The more each tries to accommodate the other, the more each unknowingly offends the other.

Another aspect of the dominance relationship is that of dependence. In the Athabaskan system, the person in the dominant position is expected to provide for others. His dependents include not only his wife and children, but also anyone in a subordinate position. In the English system, only children are considered dependents in a position to receive assistance, not any subordinates. This produces very different assumptions about what should happen in counseling, job interviews, or welfare interviews, where the petitioner is in a dependent role.

The English speaker is not really so sure of himself and so cocky about the future as he seems from the Athabaskan point of view. The Athabaskan is not as aimless and unsure of himself as he appears to be from the English point of view. These stereotyped views are the result of very predictable factors relating to the cultural expectations of the two groups. The two groups have very different views of the purpose of talking and how their goals should be accomplished through talk. These different views are closely related to the structural features of the discourse. These features are the means by which we display the attitudes and expectations we have discussed here as the presentation of self.

In the presentation of self, the English idea of "putting your best foot forward" conflicts directly with the Athabaskan observance of taboo. For English speakers, it is normal to speak as if one thinks well of himself and has high hopes for the future. Parents often say to their children, "If you don't believe in yourself, who will?" In Athabaskan society, on the other hand, it is considered bad luck to speak hopefully of the future, to say good things about yourself, or to speak badly of someone else. Thus it is inappropriate to talk about plans or play up your experience.

This difference makes it embarrassing for Athabaskan students, employees or job applicants to talk about their achievements or ambitions. English speakers in the position of teacher, employer or counselor misinterpret Athabaskan behavior as indicating lack of self-confidence and self-esteem. This misunderstanding can result in the English speaker treating the Athabaskan as if he were really aimless and unsure of himself.

When people have conversations, they have to decide who speaks first, what topics are to be talked about, how turns are exchanged, and how conversation is ended. When an Athabaskan and an English speaker talk to each other, it is a good bet that the English speaker will speak first. Considering what we have said about the presentation of self, this is not surprising. If they don't know each other well, the English speaker will start talking to find out what the Athabaskan is like, while the Athabaskan will wait to see what the other person is like.

In Western society, the person who opens a conversation has the right to introduce the topic. In Athabaskan-English conversations, since the English speaker almost always speaks first, the topic is usually controlled by the English speaker. The Athabaskan has to wait to introduce his own topic. He feels that his ideas are ignored. In office settings he often waits a long time for an opportunity to approach the English speaker so that he can be the first speaker and introduce his own topic.

The speakers in a conversation normally take turns, one person beginning after the other has finished. The pauses between the turns are accurately timed. For English speakers, after about one second, if the next speaker doesn't say anything, the first speaker can go on to say something further. Athabaskans, however, leave a longer pause between sentences than English speakers do.

In conversations between English speakers and Athabaskans, then, the English speaker pauses for about one second. If the Athabaskan does not say anything, the English speaker goes on. Meanwhile, the Athabaskan has been waiting for the English speaker to pause just an instant longer so he will not interrupt. Just when he is about to open his mouth, the English speaker starts speaking again. The Athabaskan feels that he can never get a word in edgewise, while the English speaker goes on and on.

When the Athabaskan does get the floor, he does not get a chance to say what he has to say before he is interrupted. The length of the pause he takes between sentences in one turn at talking is long enough that the English speaker thinks he is finished. The Athabaskan feels he is always being interrupted, and the English speaker feels he leaves things hanging and never makes sense.

At the end of the conversation, the English speaker feels that a departure formula is appropriate. Some simple statement like, "I'll see you later" or "I'll talk to you tomorrow" is a way of saying that the conversation was agreeable, and you expect to have a further conversation in the future. If we remember the Athabaskan caution about speaking of the future, however, we can see why such goodbyes are avoided. The Athabaskan again feels the English speaker is cocky about his expectations for the future, and the English speaker feels something went wrong in the conversation because the Athabaskan didn't even say goodbye.

We have seen how cultural expectations about the presentation of self and the mechanics of pausing and turn-taking can cause misunderstanding and ethnic stereotyping in communication between Athabaskans and English speakers. One further area of difference between them has to do with what is actually said and how it is mentally organized. Because Athabaskans and English speakers emphasize different things in speaking, both groups sometimes feel that the others do not "come right out and say" something. One example we have already looked at is that Athabaskans are not very explicit about their own accomplishments, abilities or plan, while English speakers are. Because of this, Athabaskans might feel that questions are rude, while English speakers might consider Athabaskans evasive. Another difference is the use of personal names. English speakers use them freely, while Athabaskans prefer to use titles or kin terms, which identify the right person without showing disrespect by using a personal name.

Another area that is important is the overall organization of ideas. Folktales are organized differently in the cultural traditions of the two groups. European stories have three parts, while Athabaskan stories have four. This difference shows up not only in stories, but also when people are listing items or outlining points. When Athabaskans and English speakers interact, each group feels the other is always responding at the wrong time or ignoring the main point.

When stories are told, the English speaker feels that Athabaskan stories are a little bit too long or have a section that doesn't make sense, because he expects three parts and the story has four parts. The Athabaskan might feel that the English stories leave something out, the fourth part. In conversations, they might remember different things because of different themes or organization.

Perhaps now we can see some of the reasons why each group says and feels stereotypical things about the other group. These feelings come out of what happens when they talk together. If we can understand something about how misunderstanding arises in interethnic communication, we might be less inclined to attribute misunderstanding to bad attitudes on the part of the other group. At the same time, we might be less likely to accept their stereotypes about us. Patterns of communication are very difficult to change, and change could have serious consequences for one's personal and cultural identity. The important thing is for all of us to know and understand just how we are communicating the stereotypes that others hold about us.

4. Gatekeeping

Since World War II, people have been moving around more and more. In Alaska, military bases, oil companies, the fishing industry, government agencies, and school districts have brought into contact people from many ethnic groups with different communicative styles. Alaska Natives have to deal not only with many immigrants, but also with the people they encounter to an increasing extent in national and international travels for business or pleasure.

The problems of miscommunication and negative stereotyping discussed in the previous sections are multiplied when more than two groups are involved. In corporations, education, the legal system, and state and national agencies, differences of language and communicative style must be understood and taken into account.

The social and geographical mobility of the postwar period, coupled with the concern for extending the privileges and duties of modern citizenship to all citizens, has caused multiethnic communication to become the rule rather than the exception. Exploration for energy and other resources and their distribution emphasizes arenas of political control where different modes of communication are thrust into prominence. No single group can consider its mode to be the best or only way to communicate, except in isolated instances.

In Anchorage alone, the school district is responding to the needs of students from more than fifty language groups and, we can assume, at least that many ethnic groups. Even in the typical bush settlement, there are likely to be more than two groups.

Since communicative problems rarely involve just two groups, they cannot be solved by the obvious but too simple solution that each group learn the other's code. The pervasiveness of multiple groups and multiple codes means that solutions must be sought at a level higher than that of communication between two groups.

Gatekeeping Encounters

Social, economic and geographical mobility in the modern world has meant that ways have had to be developed to control the movement of individuals into and within technological, business, educational, legal and other institutions.

Gatekeepers are individuals who have the authority to make decisions that will affect the mobility of others. They work in institutions, deciding daily whether to open the gate and let people through, or keep them out.

Counseling sessions, job and welfare interviews, and legal trials are typical gatekeeping encounters. Face-to-face interaction focused into a short time span significantly influences the life of the individual as well as the institution for some time to come. If errors in judgment are made, little can be done except arrange further gatekeeping encounters, with the risk of more of the same miscommunication.

Because of the importance of gatekeeping encounters in controlling access and mobility for institutions and determining life experiences for individuals, many institutional and legal constraints have been placed on their operation. To make these encounters as objective as possible, each gatekeeper receives equal training and briefing. Each applicant is supposed to be evaluated on a basis of equality.

Recent research by Fred Erickson has uncovered two ways in which objectivity breaks down. Where the gatekeeper and the applicant share membership in some group, whether it be a favorite sport or graduating from the same high school, there is a tendency for the applicant to fare better than applicants who do not share common ground with the gatekeeper. This sort of 'leakage' is treated as conflict of interest in the attempt to create objectivity and fairness of treatment.

The second form of leakage in gatekeeping encounters is caused by communicative style. Differences in communicative style might result in the applicant's not doing so well as one might. Some of these differences, such as length of pauses, were discussed in the previous section on ethnic stereotyping. A person's way of speaking, body placement, movement, and rhythm all affect the way what he or she says is interpreted. When these aspects of communicative style are different for gatekeeper and applicant, the gatekeeper might misinterpret what the applicant is saying, and vice versa. This might result in the very discrimination against certain applicants that the objectivity of the gatekeeping encounter is designed to prevent.

Communicative style is intimately associated with one's identity as a person and as a member of a group. Because one's own style is largely unconsciously used, leakage from communicative style is hard to put one's finger on. If it were conscious, it would be easy to acknowledge and correct, but differences in style are not conscious and corrected. Instead, people simply interpret what you do as what you intend to do. This often leads to ethnic stereotyping and negative outcomes in gatekeeping encounters.

Differences in communicative style were found between all ethnic groups in Erickson's study, but differences between members of what he called "pan-ethnic" classes of "Third World" and "white ethnic" were far greater than differences within "pan-ethnic" classes.

Ethnic stereotyping seems to operate along pan-ethnic lines. That is, Whites, Blacks, or Asians would be more likely to form stereotypes of "Alaska Natives" than of specific groups such as Athabaskans, Eskimos, or Aleuts. Therefore, we need to identify major sources of such stereotyping without necessarily describing any particular group in detail.

5. Communicative style

Now we will look more closely at aspects of communicative style, which include body movement, placement, and rhythm as well as speech. Here we will focus on discourse, by which we mean how people communicate by means of primary or basic messages and secondary or metamessages that give information about how the basic message is to be interpreted.

Problems in communication occur most often when people can tell *what* someone said, but not *why.* The metamessages that tell us *why* someone is speaking and *how* it is to be interpreted are communicated largely without the speaker's and listeners' awareness.

In looking at discourse, we are interested in untangling the interwoven strands of messages and metamessages that are part of communicative style.

We have already looked at the different ways in which Athabaskans and English speakers present themselves in public to people they do not know. Individuals present a certain 'face' to others in their society. This 'face' depends not only on a person's mood, health, or vitality, but also on the way one was brought up and one's relationships with the people one is dealing with.

Everyone has two basic desires in connection with preserving face. The positive aspect of a person's face is the concern to be thought of as a normal, contributing member of his or her society. This is the public image, the desire to be thought of as a good citizen.

At the same time, a person wants to maintain his or her autonomy, to preserve a private sphere within which one can do as one chooses without interference. This is the negative aspect of face, because it asserts the right to be independent of the social world.

In dealing with other members of society, both face wants are played off against the face wants of others, using different strategies of deference and solidarity politeness. These strategies provide a carefully calculated balance of these face wants, which are continually being negotiated in communication.

Three dimensions need to be considered in deciding which politeness strategies to use. The first is the degree of social distance or intimacy between the speaker and the hearer. The second is the power relation between them. The third is the seriousness of the communication.

People who are intimate and know each other well can say virtually anything without risking loss of face. People with a great deal of power can also say things without worrying about being polite. Some speech acts, such as asking for a match or the time of day, can be addressed to almost anyone without a great deal of fuss. Other acts need to be handled with a great deal of delicacy, especially in the presence of strangers or people who have high social status. These speech acts include joking, criticism, or requesting large sums of money.

Social anthropologists Penelope Brown and Stephen Levinson distinguish five categories of politeness strategies used in any public communication. These range from 'bald on record,' saying things without worrying about loss of face, to not saying anything because the risk is too great.

If we think about the differences in communicative style between Athabaskans and English speakers, we can see that in situations where these people are in contact, the English speakers tend toward the 'bald on record' end of the range, while Athabaskans tend toward the other extreme. Of course there are individual differences, but different ethnic groups tend to emphasize one set of strategies over others. Athabaskans might remark about certain individuals that

"She says anything," while English speakers find it more remarkable when people are habitually silent.

The second category of politeness strategies we call solidarity politeness. These strategies emphasize what the speaker and hearer have in common. They take into consideration the hearer's positive face, that is, the desire to be thought of as a supporting member of society. Solidarity politeness assumes that there is little social distance between interactants and that there is little power difference between them.

When you assume solidarity with someone, you notice and pay attention to the person, you exaggerate your interest in, approval of, and sympathy with the person; you claim in-group membership with the person, and speak as if you share a common point of view, opinions, attitudes, knowledge, and empathy. You are optimistic about your relationship, you show that you know the person's wishes and are taking them into account, and you assume or assert reciprocity.

We can now recall that in gatekeeping encounters co-membership often provides significant 'leakage' in that it improves rapport with the gatekeeper, resulting in improved access to social and institutional mobility for the applicant. We can see that co-membership emphasizes solidarity politeness strategies, decreasing distance and power differences. These strategies result in putting gatekeeper and applicant at ease, facilitating the conduct of the gatekeeping encounter in a way that favors the applicant.

Of the two basic ways of being polite or considerate to others, we have discussed solidarity, that is, showing how much you have in common with the other person. The second way is to try to keep from imposing on the other person. We call this second kind of politeness 'deference.'

Deference politeness respects the other person's right to non-interference, his right to self-determination, and to autonomy. In using deference politeness we try not to assume that we know what the other person wants or thinks or knows. We try not to speak for him or to put words in his or her mouth. We give the other person a way to avoid a difficult imposition or we even provide a way out of speaking with us. To keep from imposing, we often speak indirectly without specifically mentioning that person or ourselves. We are usually careful not to speak too much or too fast and sometimes we would rather remain silent than impose on the other person, especially if that other person is of a higher social status. We also usually avoid direct questioning.

The two styles of politeness, solidarity and deference, reflect two different underlying values. We use solidarity politeness to show respect for someone's 'positive face.' When we want to show respect for a person's public image, for a person's desire to be thought of as a good citizen, we use solidarity politeness to express our common ground and our common interest in preserving our society's values. When we want to show respect for a person's 'negative face,' we use deference. We use deference to show respect for the other person's right to non-interference and self-determination.

These two kinds of respect are both essential to normal social life. Too much of just one kind of politeness might be rude to the other person. If we stress our common ground and our common interest in society's values too strongly, we might threaten the other person's autonomy and right to self-determination. If we stress that person's right to autonomy and non-interference with too much deference, we might insinuate that the other is cold and shares nothing in common with us. In all face-to-face communication, we try to balance solidarity politeness and deference politeness. Our social institutions must always take this conflict into consideration.

If two people have somewhat different values for either self-determination or common social identity, they might severely misunderstand each other. While each is seeking to express politeness in one's own terms, the other might hear it as rudeness and might begin to develop negative stereotypes about the other. If I show too much deference to you, and you want to show me solidarity, I might think you are being pushy and violating my right to self-determination, and you might think I am cold and withdrawn or even hostile and refusing to accept the warmth and commonality you have offered. People from different ethnic groups might often misunderstand each other because of different styles of politeness that are expected in each group. While there is no group or individual that uses only solidarity politeness or only deference politeness, the balance is different from person to person, from group to group, and from situation to situation. Any two individuals in communication must try to make a balance between these two extremes.

Now we will look in more detail at how

conflict between individuals might come out of different balances in styles of solidarity and deference politeness.

6. Conflicting styles of politeness

We have talked about two different styles of politeness, deference and solidarity. Deference politeness shows respect for the other person's right to self-determination, non-interference, and autonomy. We do this by being careful not to impose our wishes on the other person, by being indirect, by not talking too much or too fast and by giving the other person every opportunity to speak or withdraw from the interaction. Solidarity politeness shows respect for the other person's right to be thought of as a good citizen, a positive contributor to society, and a friendly, likeable person. All communication tries to balance these two forms of politeness by emphasizing neither solidarity nor deference too strongly.

Misunderstanding arises because different individuals feel differently about their own self-determination or their own involvement in society. Where one person uses solidarity to emphasize his common interest with the other, and that person uses deference to emphasize non-interference, there might be a serious misunderstanding.

One might see the other as too friendly, or pushy, while the other might see the first as cold and withdrawn. Both fail to see that the other is trying to show respect through a different style of politeness.

Different ethnic groups might place different values on either group membership or individual self-determination. As a result, a member of one ethnic group might think someone from a different ethnic group with different values for politeness is rude. When this misunderstanding is allowed to go on without correction, the situation can escalate into a negative labeling of all members of that group. This can be a major source of negative ethnic stereotypes.

In gatekeeping situations such as job interviews, the 'gatekeeper,' the interviewer in this case, might make it difficult for the applicant if he uses solidarity politeness. If the applicant returns an expression of solidarity to someone in a position of higher power or status, that person could be insulted. And unfortunately, it is difficult for the applicant to know in advance just what is expected. On the other hand, if the applicant chooses to express deference politeness by being reserved in speaking, by being indirect, or by not making assumptions about the interviewer or the situation, the interviewer might think he is withdrawn, uninterested, or even hostile.

In education, for example, some researchers think that the goal of equal opportunity has led teachers to express solidarity politeness in relations with their students. This means that the teacher expresses common ground with the students and also assumes that there is little power difference or distance between them.

However, everyone knows that the teacher really does have power over the students. If the student responds to the teacher's expression of solidarity with deference, he might be punished for being dull and unresponsive. If he uses solidarity politeness, he could get in trouble for being 'pushy,' 'uppity,' or disrespectful. The only way out of this dilemma for the student is to drop out, but this is against the law.

We talked above about how some Alaska Natives express politeness. Many Alaska Natives wish to show respect to the other's right to non-interference, their self-determination, and their autonomy of personal action. They often use deference styles of politeness in a wider range of contexts than is expected by non-Natives in our society. Many Alaska Natives are careful not to speak for other individuals or to put words in their mouths. They will show respect by not making assumptions or generalizations about the other person. They will avoid bragging or talking boastfully about their own plans and ambitions.

If the 'gatekeeper' expects the 'applicant' to use solidarity politeness, he will expect the 'applicant' to emphasize common ground for their interaction. He will expect the 'applicant' to be cheerful, optimistic, and to emphasize commonly held social values.

This difference in expectations might lead to a negative evaluation of the applicant. The interviewer might think he is not really interested or actually hostile when his real intention is to show respect for the situation and the person of the interviewer. These misunderstandings may easily be translated into significant decisions that will seriously affect the future life of the applicant. Through this mechanism of misunderstood politeness, a very subtle and unconscious form of discrimination may be built into the interaction which both participants will find hard to counteract once it has begun to accumulate.

Now we would like to clarify our discussion

of styles of politeness with a partly hypothetical example of an important set of gatekeeping encounters, the legal process. The legal process consists of a series of 'gates' from the first observation of a violation of the law to the final release back into the ordinary life of a citizen, with many stages and various 'paths' through the process in between. Since this is only an example, we will not be able to treat this highly complex issue with the delicacy it deserves. Our goal is to suggest how styles of politeness may enter into the legal process as a kind of 'leakage' that produces unintended effects. We do not want to do more than suggest where problems might lie, and, if they do exist, what might be done. To provide a more careful, conscientious and accurate representation of the interactions we hypothesize here would require a major body of research that has not yet been done.

In 1978 a report of the Alaska Judicial Council suggested that for certain classes of offenses, jail sentences given in the state courts were consistently longer for Blacks and Alaska Natives than for Whites, given the same conditions of offense and prior record. The state court system, of course, has viewed this suggestion with caution and alarm: with caution because the study was based on a plea bargaining study that was not strictly and methodologically concerned with this issue, and with alarm because if this suggestion were found to be true, it might indicate serious ethnic discrimination within the state of Alaska's legal system.

The judicial system in the State of Alaska has made and continues to make every effort to limit the possibility of discrimination in the state courts. It is simply not a situation that can be dismissed as racism in the courts on the one hand or as non-existent on the other hand. In any case, the situation is not to be treated lightly, either by parties within the judicial system, or by outside observers. The potential for discrimination exists, we believe, in 'leakage' from communicative style, or as we are now in the position to discuss, from differences in the style of politeness.

We will look at only one aspect of the legal process, the pre-sentence report. The report of the judicial council noted a significant difference in the pre-sentence reports written for Native and non-Native defendants. Pre-sentence reports for Natives remarked on the absence of any expression of plans for the future. Overall these reports were said to reflect a pessimism that we associate directly with deference politeness. In contrast, both Blacks and non-Black non-Natives (a category that may include ethnic groups other than Whites) frequently expressed the intention of returning to a job or returning to school. That is, they expressed the desire to improve themselves. They put their 'best foot forward.' This expression of solidarity politeness strongly contrasts with the expression of deference politeness by Alaska Natives.

Without further analysis of the actual interactions that went into the writing of these reports, and of the reports themselves, we must be careful not to draw too many conclusions. Here we would like to suggest, though, that these expressions of solidarity politeness and deference politeness are sufficient, if everything else is equal, to produce the results reported by the judicial council.

We have suggested above that non-Natives tend to assume solidarity politeness relationships in many contexts. One of these contexts is before the law. We believe that most non-Natives assume equality before the law and that this tends to elicit expressions of solidarity politeness with representatives of the law. Alaska Natives, on the other hand, appear to assume deference relations before the law, as in many other contexts, out of respect for both individual differences and for the higher status of legal officials. While very important differences exist among Native groups and within Native groups in Alaska, in this context before the law the assumption of deference relations seems to be quite characteristic of most Native individuals. The pre-sentence reports appear to confirm this.

If the reporter expects expressions of solidarity politeness, but the defendant uses deference politeness, this might appear to the reporter as withdrawal, lack of ambition and future plans, or even hostility. This negative evaluation could be reflected in pre-sentence reports that suggest negative personal characteristics.

In the legal process there are more and less formal contexts. This difference is important because most individuals will show deference politeness in highly formal contexts such as the court itself, but the variation between individuals is much greater in less formal contexts. We believe that the pre-sentence report might reflect a conflict in style of politeness in one of the less formal legal contexts.

The court itself is a system where deference politeness is expected by virtually all participants. There is a high power difference and high distance respected among all participants. The appropriate interactive decorum calls for deference to the authority of the court. We believe that most defendants from all minority groups understand this and in fact display the appropriate deference <u>while in court</u>.

The problem that surfaces in the pre-sentence reports lies between the original arrest and the court. The pre-sentence report is prepared not in court, but in a somewhat less awesome, less formal context. The individuals involved in preparing these reports might not be in the formal position to command deference politeness within the American legal system. These individuals might frequently operate from the basic assumption of solidarity politeness. They tend to show warmth, common social identity, and respect for the defendant's common social purpose. Whatever is actually said, it is interpreted as optimism, 'putting your best foot forward,' and might well be recorded in the language of solidarity politeness. This, in turn, expresses the underlying assumption of all parties of equality before the law, which is heard, of course, as respect for the law, respect for the legal system. This at least supports if not fosters a favorable outcome in court.

On the other hand, the deference politeness that is often shown by Alaska Natives to strangers or in situations of stress is expressed as making very few assumptions about the outcomes and rather full submission to the wishes of the other party, in this case the law. This might be heard by those preparing pre-sentence reports as an expression of lack of enthusiasm, withdrawal, or even hostility or guilt. This deference politeness might sound like acceding power to the individual preparing the report, which might result in some all-too-human exaggeration of the potential for the expression of power. This misperception of the polite deference of Natives might reflect itself in a report language of indifference, shiftlessness, or strong assumptions of guilt. This sort of report could easily be translated into a more severe sentence than one expressing the assumed optimism of solidarity politeness.

The problem that underlies this misunderstanding is the reporter's assumption of commonality before the law coupled with the Native's assumption of respect for the distance between himself and the reporter. Both are acting out of respect and concern for each other, but the means of expression 'backfires' and produces quite contrary messages. It is at least possible that such reports could influence the sentencing process.

Some of the factors that enter into this potential for discrimination through communicative style can now be identified. The first factor is the assumption individuals might have about basic styles of politeness. Where these are differently balanced there is the potential for conflict. The second factor is assumptions individuals make about the legal process, solidarity politeness out of court, deference politeness within court. A third factor surfaces which should be considered in further research, the role of the non-professional in non-formal contexts. One researcher found that in a large hospital, while policy prevented discrimination by hospital staff, decisions by ambulance drivers in approaching the emergency entrance affected the outcomes for the emergency patients they were delivering. Some patients were delivered with great urgency, including the sounding of the ambulance siren. Others were delivered slowly, with only the honk of the horn. The latter were treated with less urgency by the receiving staff. It was significant that those latter cases tended to be members of minority groups, the aged, or patients obviously under the influence of alcohol. An informal and unofficial decision by the ambulance driver was significant in determining what sort of treatment individuals would receive as patients in a public hospital.

We have taken the position in these notes that multi-ethnic communication is a fact of the modern world. We see no reason why or how this should change in the predictable future. We have identified a significant situation, the gate-keeping encounter, in which there is a serious potential for discrimination against ethnic or other social groups by those who hold institutional, social, or economic or technological power. We have argued that the most serious potential for discrimination lies in 'leakage' into the situation from differences in communicative style. Communicative style we have seen as consisting partly of patterns of discourse, the ways in which speech and verbal interaction are integrated. While discourse consists of at least the distribution of talk, the information structure, cognitive frames, schema and scripts, and the presentation of self through talking, we have seen the latter, the presentation of self, as the key to understanding interethnic communication.

The problem that we would like to discuss is how differences in assumptions about styles of politeness can be reconciled in a multiethnic institutional framework. In both the comments we have made on education and in the example above of the judicial system, complications arose from the fact that one party had assumed a style of solidarity politeness while the other had assumed a style of deference politeness as the appropriate way to show respect for the situation. In other words, one party chose to emphasize the common grounds for interaction, while the other party chose to emphasize fundamental differences between individuals. There is an overriding problem with solidarity politeness. Solidarity politeness carries with it the potential for creating a double bind. In gatekeeping situations, one party has been invested with the power to make decisions that have serious impact on the lives of the applicants at the 'gate.' If the gatekeeper uses solidarity politeness, it might be heard doubly, either as an expression of power, or as an expression of common grounds or solidarity. As we have said above, co-membership will override ethnic difference in such encounters. The applicant is in a double bind. He is enticed into solidarity expressions by the hope that co-membership will work to his advantage. In using solidarity politeness, he risks sounding disrespectful of the power of the gatekeeper. If he uses deference politeness, he risks sounding withdrawn, unconcerned, hostile, or haughty, and thereby jeopardizes his chances of success.

We believe that only the gatekeeper is in the position to remove the double bind, having access as he does to the sources of power and decision that control the situation. The only way to untie the double bind of interethnic gatekeeping encounters is for the gatekeeper to use deference politeness voluntarily. In other words, the gatekeeper must avoid expressions of solidarity, of common social purpose. He must cultivate a respect for the applicant's right to non-interference, self-determination, and autonomy of action. The gatekeeper must assume a responsibility for understanding, accepting, and positively valuing the differences presented by the applicants. Further intensification of the expression of solidarity relations by gatekeepers in multi-ethnic situations can only be interpreted as a wish to increase the double bind into which the power of the gatekeeper has placed the applicant.

We can see then that at the level of world communication the way to improve communication is not to adopt some common language such as English, 'Basic English,' 'Standard English,' or any other 'standard' form of language, or in fact any means of communication predicated on commonness of education or experience. Because of the complexity of world communication, we also cannot expect solutions based on everyone's learning everyone else's communicative system or style of politeness. Even within Alaska the degree of complexity is too great for this type of solution. The only viable solution that we can advance is the cultivation of an international, interethnic, intercultural communicative style of deference politeness. We must assume at the foundation that communication is difficult and problematical, that we must minimize our impositions on others, that we must leave others the option of not acting on our impositions or acting as they choose, and that we can make only minimal assumptions about the wants, needs, relevancies, and priorities of others. The only common ground on which interethnic communication can be based without discrimination is a recognition of the value of difference and a respect for it.

Recommendations for Improved Interethnic Communication

There are three basic steps toward improving interethnic communication.

Perception. We need to perceive that our communication is not entirely successful.

Acceptance. We need to accept that others do not intend to convey wrong or confusing information or to convey negative attitudes.

Repair. We need to seek ways of explicitly sorting out how and where communication goes wrong.

It is very important to realize that each of us has learned his or her communicative style or styles as part of our personal and social identity. It is very difficult to focus directly on the attitudes we communicate and when it comes down to it, no one else can do it for us.

Learning how to communicate effectively in interethnic communication situations can only come out of practice and learning in those situations.

1. Listen until the other person is finished. Very often we cut people off before they have reached their main point. If we cut them off too soon, there is the danger that they will feel we are rude and that we will feel they do not make any sense. When people have different communicative styles, they have different senses of timing. More patient listening can help with this problem.

2. Allow extra time. If we are going to let people have their say, it might take more time to accomplish group tasks or interviews or other communications. We believe that the extra time taken right then and there is more than made up for in the time saved later that might be otherwise wasted in confusion or having to go over everything again from the beginning. This time is also being spent in learning others' ways of communicating and is being well spent.

3. Avoid "crowded" situations. Try to communicate one-to-one whenever possible. It is much easier for two people to adjust to each other than a larger group. It has been found that an individual's reaction time may be much faster in a group than speaking one-to-one. To allow for more leisurely accommodation, it is best to avoid communicating in large groups.

4. Talk openly about communication. It is uncomfortable to focus on communication, but unless we learn to do this, we will not learn how we are being misunderstood. Your 'interethnic partner' has everything to gain by a mutual attention to the process of communication itself, and we cannot learn how we are being misunderstood until we talk to someone who sees it differently.

5. Talk openly about discrimination. For members of ethnic minorities, discrimination is often the main concern in communication, but it is a very difficult subject to bring up. Non-minority group members can help the situation by showing a willingness to consider that they might be acting in ways that produce discrimination.

6. Seek help. Seek out sympathetic individuals from other ethnic groups who are willing to discuss communicative problems with you. A concerned friend can tell you more than any number of experts in communication. It is very important, however, not to indulge in same-group rehashes of the ways of other ethnic groups. Whether these are ethnic jokes, negative epithets, or even concerned attempts to understand "them," there is a very great danger that talking in terms of "us" and "them" will only reinforce stereotypes that are already held by your own group about others. Your best information will come from someone who is very different from you. You should seek out those individuals, offer your attempt to understand in exchange for their help in understanding yourself.

7. Learn to expect and appreciate difference. Communication in the modern world is complex. We cannot expect solutions to communication problems based on everyone learning everyone else's communicative system. The only viable solution is for each to understand his or her own system and to respect the fact that others will often be very different, and that those differences will complicate communication. We must assume at the foundation that communication is difficult and problematical. We must minimize our impositions on others and leave others the option of not acting on our impositions, or of acting as they choose. We must make minimal assumptions about the wants, needs, relevancies, and priorities of others. The only common ground on which interethnic communication can be based without discrimination is a recognition of the value of difference and a respect for it.

Suggestions for further reading:

Interethnic Communication is based on the material in Chapter Two, "Athabaskan-English Interethnic Communication," of our book *Narrative, Literacy, and Face in Interethnic Communication* (Norwood, New Jersey: Ablex Publishing Corporation, 1981). That book contains much more detail as well as a full bibliography of references.

For practical suggestions on how to improve communication, see our book *Responsive Communication: Patterns for Making Sense* (Haines, Alaska: The Black Current Press, 1986). Responsive Communication contains fifty patterns that we have used as the basis for workshops and interactional training.